RAIN 'EM UP

# tell me about
# GRACE

created by
## STEPHEN ELKINS

*illustrated by*
## RUTH ZEGLIN & SIMON TAYLOR-KIELTY

Tyndale House Publishers, Inc.
Carol Stream, Illinois

wonder
kids
Songs to Inspire Faith

choo choo,
choo choo!
choo choo!

# ALL ABOARD!

## All aboard the Gospel train!

# Get on Board, Little Children

FIND THIS SONG on the CD

The gospel train is comin'
The wheels go 'round and 'round
We're training up the children
So they'll be heaven bound

### Chorus
Get on board, little children
Get on board, little children
Get on board, little children
There's room for many a-more

Hear that train a-comin'
Comin' down the track
I'll be getting on it
And won't be lookin' back

### Repeat chorus

You won't need a penny
To ride this glorious train
Just give your heart to Jesus
And ride away with Him

### Repeat chorus

Have you ever wondered what

# GRACE is?

welcome to
**BIBLE LAND**

*Yes, I have!*
**What IS GRACE?**

We're off to
**DISCOVERY LAND**
to find the answer.

Let's discover what the Bible says about

# GRACE!

**1 Mile**

**DISCOVERY LAND**

Some people think **GRACE** is

# SOMETHING

we believe in.

But the Bible says that **GRACE** is

# SOMEONE

we believe in. And that someone is Jesus Christ!

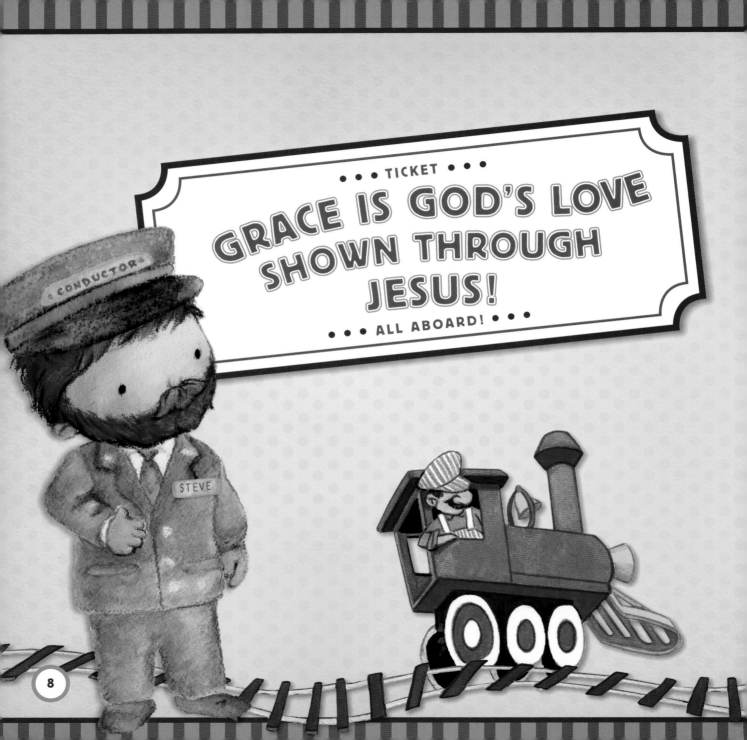

TICKET

GRACE IS GOD'S LOVE SHOWN THROUGH JESUS!

ALL ABOARD!

CONDUCTOR

STEVE

8

**Sometimes** what you **don't** see is more important than what you **do** see. We might see a train chugging down the tracks. But what we don't see is the powerful engine that drives the train.

Grace is like that unseen engine. We see Jesus buried and risen to new life. But God's unseen GRACE is the power that raised Him from the dead to new life! Even though God is unseen, His love and His grace became visible at the cross!

..............................................................................

*May our Lord Jesus Christ himself and God our Father, who loved us and by his grace gave us eternal comfort and a wonderful hope, comfort you and strengthen you in every good thing you do and say.*
**2 THESSALONIANS 2:16-17**

GOD'S GRACE became visible at the CROSS!

GRACE is God's FAVOR.

**W**HEN WE ARE SAVED, we receive a great gift: God's complete forgiveness and acceptance! He no longer sees the bad things we have done. Nor does He see the bad things we may do!

When He looks at us, He sees only Jesus! Because of Him, we are forgiven and accepted forever! Even though we deserve to be separated from God, He gives us just the opposite! For the gift of God is eternal life, love, and acceptance!

. . . . . . . . . . . . . . . . . . . . . . . . . . . . . . . . . . . . . . . . . . . . . .

*God always gives you all the grace you need.*

**1 PETER 5:10, NIrV**

GRACE AND MERCY are like two sides of the same coin. God shows GRACE by giving us something we **DON'T** deserve. God shows MERCY by **NOT** giving us what we **DO** deserve: separation from Him.

It's like a judge who pays the fine a guilty man owes. Then, he sets the man free even though the man is guilty. Grace is God giving us eternal life even though we do not deserve it. Grace and mercy both come from God!

............................................................

*Let us come boldly to the throne of our gracious God. There we will receive his mercy, and we will find grace to help us when we need it most.*

**HEBREWS 4:16**

**W**E ARE SAVED by **GOD'S** GRACE, and nothing else. God alone is **able** to save us. God alone is **able** to wash away our sins. He alone is **able** to keep us going, no matter what the day may bring. It is not our power, but the engine of His GRACE!

Grace is an unseen power given to Christians. It gets us through tough times. It's the strength we need to endure disappointment. God's grace is able to save!

. . . . . . . . . . . . . . . . . . . . . . . . . . . . . . . . . . . . . . . . . . . . . . . . . . . . . . .

*God is able to make every grace overflow to you, so that in every way, always having everything you need, you may excel in every good work.*

**2 CORINTHIANS 9:8,** HCSB

WE ARE SAVED by GRACE. We don't earn it by working hard or singing a great song. We aren't saved because we attend church every Sunday or give to the poor. These are all good things, but they are things WE do.

GRACE is something GOD does. He gives grace to us as a gift! We don't earn it; we receive it as a gift from our heavenly Father!

. . . . . . . . . . . . . . . . . . . . . . . . . . . . . . . . . . . . . . . . . . . . . . . . . . . . .

*God saved you by his grace when you believed. And you can't take credit for this; it is a gift from God.* **EPHESIANS 2:8**

THE APOSTLE PAUL had a problem. We are not sure what is was. He called it a "thorn in the flesh." I once got a thorn in my finger and it really hurt! Maybe Paul had an illness or a disease.

Paul asked God to remove this "thorn." But each time God answered, "No. My grace is able to keep you strong. My power is made perfect in weakness." Grace is the power! Grace is the engine that keeps us strong when we are weak!

# GRACE KEEPS YOU STRONG

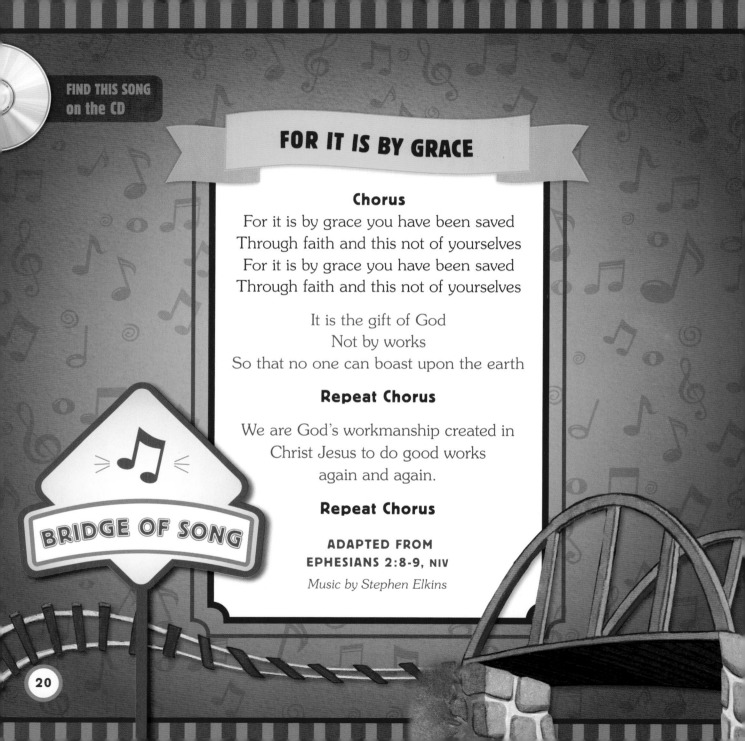

**FIND THIS SONG**
**on the CD**

# FOR IT IS BY GRACE

### Chorus

For it is by grace you have been saved
Through faith and this not of yourselves
For it is by grace you have been saved
Through faith and this not of yourselves

It is the gift of God
Not by works
So that no one can boast upon the earth

### Repeat Chorus

We are God's workmanship created in
Christ Jesus to do good works
again and again.

### Repeat Chorus

**ADAPTED FROM
EPHESIANS 2:8-9, NIV**

*Music by Stephen Elkins*

**BRIDGE OF SONG**

## WHAT DID YOU LEARN ABOUT GRACE? *(answers at bottom of page)*

1. Grace shows God's _____.

2. Grace shows God's _____.

3. Grace shows God's _____.

4. Grace shows God is _____.

5. Grace is a _____.

LEARNING STATION

1. favor, 2. mercy, 3. love, 4. able, 5. gift

The Bible says that **JESUS** was full of **GRACE.**
Do you believe that?

.......................................................

Do you believe God's grace is able to **SAVE US?**

.......................................................

Do you believe that grace is the **GIFT** of God?

.......................................................

Do you believe that gift is given to **YOU?**

.......................................................

Would you like to **RECEIVE**
God's grace by **FAITH?**

DECISION DEPOT

**LORD, hear us when we PRAY:**

## HEAVENLY FATHER,

I love You. You alone are able to forgive my sins. You alone are able to free me from their power.

You have told me that Jesus was full of grace. I believe it! Because of Him, I receive what I do not deserve: forgiveness and your blessing of eternal life. Because of Jesus, I do not receive the penalty of sin I do deserve. Thank You, Father, for Your amazing grace! *Amen.*

**PRAYER PLACE**

# TRAIN UP A CHILD

Train up, train up,
Train up a child in the way he should go.
Train up, train up,
Train up a child in the way she should go.
And when they are older
They will not depart from it.

**ADAPTED FROM
PROVERBS 22:6**

*Words & music by Stephen Elkins*

I know the LORD must love all this great singing!
## And He loves you, too!
**Last stop! Good-bye, everybody.** *See you next time
when once again we'll choo-choo away
aboard the Gospel train and discover
all that God has for us!*